MISSISSIPPI DELTA WOMEN IN PRISM

Anne, Jim said you are a
poet also! We need to talk!
I love Jim as a very good friend.
He is so supportive of
writers.   Love,   1/15/02
Claire

MISSISSIPPI DELTA WOMEN IN PRISM

POEMS BY
Claire T. Feild

COURT STREET PRESS

Montgomery

Court Street Press
P.O. Box 1588
Montgomery, AL 36102

Library of Congress Cataloging-in-Publication Data

ISBN 1-58838-038-6

Design by Randall Williams
Printed in the United States of America

WITH LOVE TO MY HUSBAND

HUBERT S. FEILD, JR.

AND TO OUR SON

TAYLOR SPOTTSWOOD FEILD

WITH RESPECT TO MY DECEASED PARENTS

JAMES CLAUDE "BROWNIE" TAYLOR

AND GWENDOLYN S. TAYLOR-JOHNSON,

WITH FONDNESS TO

RU-DUD

WHO INSPIRED ME TO WRITE CREATIVELY

Kudzu Animals

Towering above the hills, the kudzu animals'
dark green eyes guard Highway 49, a roller
coaster that beams white for thirteen miles or
so before it stops short, out of steam, letting
Broadway Street make the final descent to the
Mississippi Delta.

What the highwaymen steal from the kudzu
animals is more than an eye here or there—
but their progeny, the smallest forms that
have tried to wrap themselves into cradle
leaves, their parents slanted arms.

The children are the first to go, their roots
tumbling, trembling in the hot breeze from
the highwayman's slash.

Some say the Delta begins too soon;
flattened green pinioned so low that
the everlasting fields of soft cotton
seem like deformed offspring from the
glint of czar green.

HISTORICAL NOTE: When I was a child growing up in Yazoo City, Mississippi, in the 1950s, the deep green kudzu-shaped animals near Highway 49 were my friends. Riding to Yazoo City years ago, I looked forward to reuniting with my childhood friends. To my dismay, they were gone, having become an environmental nuisance to others.

Contents

IV. Faith in Freedom / 103

Preface

I was born and grew up in Yazoo City, Mississippi, the town where the hills meet the Mississippi Delta. Although I grew up there in the 1950s and early sixties, a time when the status quo for women of color and otherwise was established, I distinctly remember as a very young child staring at my mother, who was washing dishes, and thinking, "Is this what women do?" Taking inventory at Henick's Auto Supply with my daddy appealed to me at the time.

Thus, I grew up from the beginning thinking, without being told, that Mississippi Delta women were not free. Unfortunately, I lived in "the Closed Society," so I never realized then that most, if not all women, were also not free to achieve their dreams without feeling that they had somehow done something improper.

So, it is with great respect for all women at that time and place, whether they stood anywhere on the continuum that progressed from women of guise, still not free, or women of strength, still not free, that I wrote *Mississippi Delta Women in Prism* because whatever I see through and learn from the Mississippi Delta women of the 1950s and early sixties, is a distortion of the way life is for me now and for so many other women living today.

Acknowledgments

Some of the poems in this volume have been previously published and/or have been honored with prizes. Grateful acknowledgment is paid to the respective publications and contests as follows:

"Kudzu Animals," *Noccalula*, 1998; "Bubba and His Horse-Drawn Carriage," nominated for Pushcart Prize by *Krater Quarterly*, 2001; "A Spring Tea," *Bloodstone Stanislaus Poetry Anthology*, 1999, and *Aura Literary Arts Magazine*, 1999; "Pralines," *Shatter the Glass Ceiling*, 1998; "Longing," *Shatter the Glass Ceiling*, 1998; "Stilted," *Wired Art from Wired Hearts*, 2000; "Sultry," Grey Book Press, 2001; "Overload," *DAYbreak*, 1999; "Cursive," *Barefoot Grass Journal*, 1997; "The Dance," *Poets Corner*, 1998; "The Washboard," *Crone Chronicles: A Journal of Conscious Aging*, 2000; "Delta Clover," *Sophie's Wind*, 2000; "Finality," *Mediphors: A Literary Journal of the Health Professions*, 2000; "Walter," *Wired Art from Wired Hearts*, 2000; "The Doorman," *Sophie's Wind*, 2000; "The Ice House," *Art:Mag*, 2000; "The Yazoo River," *The Guild*, 2001; "The Conjurer," *American Writing: A Magazine*, 1999; "The Boarding House," *Footsteps*, 2000; "The Message," *Buffalo Woman's Vision*, 2002; "Finding the Key," *Big Muddy: A Journal of the Mississippi River Valley*, 2002; "Ennui," *Red River Review*, 2000; "Cold Colloquy," *The Neovictorian/Cochlea*, 1999; "Brickyard Hill," *The Mending Wall*, 2000, and *Noccalula*, 1997; "Ruby Red," *The*

Eclectic Woman, Sweet Annie and Sweet Pea Press, 1997; "The Tent Revival," *Architrave,* 1999; "The Iconoclast," *Nebo: A Literary Journal,* 1998; "The Apology," *Olden Times,* Sweet Annie and Sweet Pea Press, 1996; "The Adventure," *Indigenous Fiction,* 1999; "Sisters," Honorable Mention, Genevieve F. Kallander Award, Mississippi Spring Contest, 1997; "Pilaf," *Buffalo Woman's Vision,* 2002; "Memory," *DAYbreak,* 2001; "Handcuffed," *Folio: A Literary Journal of American University,* 2001; "God's Acre," *Parnassus Literary Journal,* 2001; "Evenness of Tone," *IdioM,* 2001; "Digression," *Wired Art from Wired Hearts,* 2000; "Danseuse," *DAYbreak,* 2001; "Another Side," *Smartish Pace,* 2000; "One with Shade," *The Neovictorian/Cochlea,* 2001; "A Bouquet of Glads," *Sophie's Wind,* 2000; "The Kitchen Sink Glass," *Apostrophe: USCB Journal of the Arts,* 2000; "The Delta Queen," *Noccalula,* 1998; "Sinewy," *Goddessing Regenerated,* 2002; "Shearing," *IdioM,* 2001; "Cream of the Crop," *Noccalula,* 1998; "Incognito," *The Sunday Suitor Poetry Review,* 1997; "Ignescent," *MM Review's Annual Anthology,* 1999; "Chemise," *Potpourri: A Quarterly International Magazine,* 2002; "A Readiness for Life," *Buffalo Woman's Vision,* 2001.

1

THE PROPRIETIES

White Patent Leather Shoes

Her black nose, flattened against The Black and White
Store window, had the breath of an enlarged eye floater.
The pair of shoes that flourished her thoughts looked like a
flat piece of white paper, yet shimmered like what she guessed
a petrified piece of wood would look like in her own hands.
Although the shoes were a delicacy to her, her mother thought
them flimsy as white society at its diaphanous teas
and sheer church meetings.

The patriarch read her daughter's thoughts as if they were
stationed within her own mind to the point of fermenting there.
"No, the white shoes would not be appropriate for our kind."
To the child, however, color would remain bald.

Bubba and His Horse-Drawn Carriage

Aunt Ludie loved feigning to be ill, and everyone
knew it in the tackled community where she lived,
making fun of her behind her back that she likened
to a constant leg cramp.
Her "arthritic" fingers were smooth, long, and
flexible as a chameleon's long green tail.
Her head throbbed at the grandfather clock's cue:
the chime she heard every fifteen minutes when
she lay on the porch's yellow divan in mourning
over her conditions.
After she called her doctor, he brought his stethoscope
but waved it back and forth like a pendulum while
she described her pains.
Aunt Ludie knew of only one person who would
take her seriously, and it was Bubba.

Bubba's head and body might look like a ganglion cyst
while he drove his horse-drawn carriage, but he
had an aura of kosher that most admired.
When Aunt Ludie dialed his number, she already
knew he would come get her, take her to the
hospital in style.
As Aunt Ludie proudly took her seat in the carriage,
Bubba looked sick to her, but she would never know
that his shyness about telling her the truth made him
draw up into a nothingness equal to the force of
Aunt Ludie's manifestations.

A Spring Tea

Precise and secure she stands, her stomach flat, not from
a corset, but from the warm reminder within that to be
accepted by the women she emulates, she must position
herself the way the elderly used to, but can't now because
of numerous pastries they consumed at other teas just like
this one.
She stirs the yellow punch completely.
(heaven forbid she stir vigorously, for she would be called common)
She thinks its yellow color a flaccid imitation of the Delta
sun, a rotunda in the sky,
and the punch's ice cubes, the only coldness these women
will ever experience, their deep laughter between sips keeping
their minds tepid with the belief that what they do on a spring
afternoon is more important than any other activity in their
community, their vocalizations wrenching the dirt from
so in so about *so in so,* then feeling cleansed in the process,
at peace with themselves because they are unlike the uninvited
ones, frankly just too good for them anyway.
Her purple gown scratches, but she will endure this minor
inconvenience, for the punch bowl looks like the giant
chandelier she will eventually inherit when she marries
the talk of the town, and the crystal cups will be the ones
her children will fill for her friends on other Delta spring
afternoons that had better not deviate from this one *one iota.*

The Jewelry Case

When she stares at Mama's jewelry case, its
black-shellacked background disappears, and a
clear revelation appears: Japanese women wearing
bold-faced kimonos, yet tilling the fields with
hands that seem to slide from the rakes, hands
looking softer than silk dresses gently falling
from closet hangers, steamy from the heat
that rappels from ceiling to floor in each room
of her home.

But the droll, yet compliant mystery surfaces
for the umpteenth time.
Why does the Cuban case have Japanese
women toiling on its many faces?
Did a Cuban artisan-gentleman marry a Japanese
lady?
Confusion also rules the case's black tassels
she wants to liberate one by one, the elongated
dominoes falling with style.
She recoils at the thought of the touch of a tassel;
Mama's secrets might fly out, never to return.

Exchanging Peter for Paul

Since Aunt Etoile's home was as large
as a double-exposed monastery and
she had nothing better to do than wear
her pink scuffs and baby blue robe all day,
she conjured up the word *change* from
a society that was bent on sending that
word and its connotations to the bottom
of rivers where the black folks once lay.

So a picture of a dark-haired woman dressed
in a soft beige gown and playing a piano
near winding stairs was taken from its place
and moved to the place where a deer head
perched from a wall's thicket of atrocities.
Since Aunt Etoile had made switches to spank
her dolls when she was a tyke, switching things
was as natural to her as behavior she deemed
appropriate to keep her dolls aristocratic.

When the maid Puree (she was called Puree
because she kept a giant red freckle on her
nose) asked Aunt Etoile why she had been born
for the purpose of changing things, Aunt Etoile
swirled her robe from the wooden floor's creases,
kicked her scuffs to kingdom come, then
replied, *"Why, the only way to stay wealthy
is to trade Peter for Paul."*

Exquisite

Her wan features and thoughts curve
and wrinkle *just so* . . . she's a sheet of baklava
snug-fitting one of the dining room's high-backs.

Her spine straight as *Bacillus*, she sits
inside a flowing dress, the color and shape of
an upside tulip, yet the ingrained mores
that have been drilled into her mind
are contagious, even to those who will
stalk around clueless as her progeny.

So she pans the ceiling for the sight of
blue, pretending her cover is the sky
instead of the place she must occupy
each time she eats, dove like, a kept
lady inside gruel, afraid of being
cross-grained from a touch of smudge.

Pralines

Expressionless, she stands at the white gate, quietly poised,
surveying the distant white faces, snowballs thrown into
a time they would like to dismiss but can't because. . .
the she,
the starched apron,
and the red bandana
won't let them.
They buy her pralines willingly, for that's the proper
act of courtesy.
But they don't look into her sharp brown eyes
for fear that in their depths a fatal truth about
themselves will emerge,
and they might have to strangle genealogy's brutish
whispers that image, "Let the past live on."
So thy pass her gentle form and embrace the remains of
an antebellum home one last time before they pretend it
slithers down a degenerate bluff into the Mississippi River's
staunch clutch, the past's pallid propriety engulfed by the grand equalizer.

The Sacred Rule

When she confidently opened the door, announcing meekly
she would remarry,
the room and its inhabitants imploded,
speechless,
thinking she had taken a Cook's tour and was falsely impressed.
"All that glitters is not gold," her best friend copycat-
penned in a lengthy letter.
But she needed the money—
a daughter to send to college,
a woman who had not pursued her dreams in a society
so meticulously constant
that the slightest deviation from its sacred rule of
subordination would ignite a role war between the sexes.
The chilly stillness,
the frozen responses,
the relatives unable to guide her to
independence—
their world having trained her to be dependent.

Longing

Sitting down but clawing the chair's arms, she
tends present time.
She hears a lilting note, a reminder of events
that used to satisfy
and could settle her now
if she were not sabotaged by a
stern time.
Changes sauntering,
gradually replacing
what was comfortable,
what she had hoped would last forever
but knew couldn't,
so that a new generation of pygmies
would have the room for a short time too.

Stilted

They stand precariously in the reckless shadows,
closed boxes in a mosquito-infested locale—
the tepid summer nights sequestered
by the Delta's clutch.
The dark water swirls,
then splashes against
the houses' long, gradually deteriorating
legs
that neither flinch
nor move forward,
but just put change
on hold for the young ones
superimposed upon a
staid culture,
whose hoop skirts
prevent the changing of the
guard.

HISTORICAL NOTE: Houses owned by poor blacks in the 1950s in Yazoo City, Mississippi, were on stilts because water ran below the houses there when the river flooded. The houses are still there, providing a dire entranceway to cotton fields.

Sultry

When the Delta sun melted the
twelve ice cubes, miniature havens
for those suffering from the heat
waves that penetrated the land, just
as beach waves do the shore,
Grand Avenue sizzled, its lusty
steam rising upward, coalescing
into a coltish, yet poorly designed
dirigible, moving forward like a
snail, in a place and time when
ardent emotions wore overcoats,
and the coals underneath huff-
smoldered, dreading the
inevitable collisions that would
birth a new order, the ghostly
loafers in the lobby still toasting, the
tinkling of their glasses stilled.

Chenille

When Chenille went to a tea or church
or rambled around in Woolworth's, she
wore silk dresses, for she thought to be
cup-measured proper, a portion of silk
dress should be touching land, a dirty
brown wooden shop floor, or anything
else she considered as stable as she was.
Although most of the elderly town
residents shivered at the thought that her
behavior was right next door to odd, they
uttered few comments about this protrusion
into what was referred to as a silent lecture
about how they should be: pure to the core.

So Chenille became their goddess,
untouchable, and a yardstick by which
they could measure how close they came
to riding in perfection's saddle.

The day Chenille died, her clothes closet
that sequestered a permanent rainbow
was open to the public's scrutiny. But there
was another unknown closet that had to be
opened by a locksmith, a tired old man
whose keys had unlocked secrets best left
alone like yellow jackets. As the locksmith
opened Chenille's other closet for the nosy
ones, the ones whose weak souls fluttered
at the end of gossamer threads, a closet
full of gunnysacks stared at them, thick
brown ghosts telling them what she had
been and what they would always be.

Old Maids

When they straight-set across the sticky, unbalanced
cardboard table from each other, their forms shrieked
the word *proud*, even though they had nothing
except each other, and that was too much.

Mirror images of each other now, a ringworm
scorn had not always been there. Since one lady
had been brighter and prettier than the other one
during youth's throes, she could not accept the
demise in her own looks, so kicked unmercifully
at the other one's long fleshy leggings.

But the scrubbed one never moved, for the
slightest motion on her part would be just
one more defeat added to the ones she had
accumulated throughout the years, the memory
of them stuck within a goblet cobweb ripening,
ready to turn over in her head, casting her into
a gracious oblivion.

Overload

Her mind,
each neuron firing,
scrambling for a front row seat
in the amphitheater.
Her mind,
a precious hieroglyph.
When full with stereotypical thoughts
and an aversion to a complex novelty,
it closes dead shut.
In fear, her body moves through space
but not with the times.
Her frozen mind wears an overcoat
of red snow.
If an auger could bore a hole
through the icy foothold
and let the poisons escape,
her fear of overload would no longer
be an issue.
The illimitable could play its
trump card.

Lydia

The lady was paler than a snowflake
that melts into a cool nothingness.
But she still dusted her chalky white
totality with talcum powder so the
rages within, the ones that tried to
summon a manifest destiny, could
occasionally be stilled.

When she tread to the dark corner
of her freckled-with-light bedroom,
like nursing home patients drag the
slippers they wear, all instinctively
proclaimed that it was quiet time for
the lady, the one who would later
scramble around in a yellow-bellied
reality, trying to gobble up, to no
avail, what had always been set
before her, a society on automatic
pilot, the proprieties continuously
settling in, rubbing rules deep into
a wan society.

Cursive

The night's dark, tweedless tendrils swishing lightly,
brush the day's intense heat under a thick carpet
of black.
Sitting underneath a weeping willow tree, boys tell
cool stories about swampy characters who yearn for a
hayride with Magnolia girls, totaled sweet, but when
confronted with the dilemma of a meltdown, have no
conical depth,
their opinions easily re-cycled,
their good looks mussed inside pink, plastic containers.

The Dance

My father, the Pale Horse
my mother, definitive—
"It's just not the proper thing, going to a dance,
your father's just passing."
"But Mother, my daddy would want me to go. If he
were here, he'd tell you that."
Irresolute, Mother summons an ultimatum from the
place where the sins of the Fathers squeeze out a
vicious feel from one of uncommon carriage.
"I guess I'm just going to have to call the minister
to get him to reason with you."
The child, more woman than some, climbs into her bed,
sucking her pinky, wishing she were at school, where
she could pretend her daddy upright, the Cro-Magnon
man at his evolutionary best.
A bald-headed man wearing a slick brown suit and matching
tie strides confidently into her room, craning meekly
over devastation, but just goody-two-shoes happy to be
doing the correct thing.

The Washboard

When I watched her scrub my undies, the warm wind
blowing from the open kitchen window caused my
head to turn upwards, to realize that her wavy black
hair looked just like the washboard's wooden grooves.

When I stood on a chair to equalize our relationship,
I later learned that I had accomplished the improbable
in a society where falsifications stayed seated within
the larger order of events.

While I moved my index finger up and down each wavelet,
I felt that I could be a part of something dark and be right—
until she slammed my spell glass into a million kickshaws
by a reflex utterance:
"Now child, what you doing standing up here so close to me?
If Mama see you, she going to bring out the switch."

Delta Clover

When night's blacktop road
folds within the sun's portal,
infinitesimal water cups
in our world
lounge undisturbed atop
untamed clover platters
that later split wide open in the
heat of noon.
Decorum's force is not here—

But in the distance, late afternoon
ladies girdled within air-thin rainbow
gowns and starched petticoat puffs,
toss golden pennies toward the
foot of the fountain's harsh terrain.

A purple cloud, shackled, takes
shallow breaths,
then rumbles cautiously.
The tired ladies ignore its shy
admonitions *now*.
Engaged in small talk,
the ladies' words are
the husk of a deeper
consciousness that will
be felt in their offspring.

The Debutante

When she stood before the oval, full-length mirror,
what she saw was designed, contoured to fit perfectly
over the silhouettes of other beauty queens content
to suffocate in the town's warm silt.
Knowing that she was pretty, having been first lady
at a fitting, she felt glad to be part of the fission of
the known and very much respected one who had
made it possible for her to be a whole organism
alongside her special friend from childhood.
She reveled in the fact that a Renaissance man
had been chosen for her by her principled parents.

On the pad that lay on her dresser, she took a
well-meaning delight in drawing minus signs, for
she did not want to know herself.
Why should *she* be the one to usher in a new fugue
when she would be her man's embodiment of fertility.

Finality

Bright light robes the anterior queen,
the bed, her life's frame now.
Grasped by misery's tongs,
she curls up,
a lacey green roly-poly
with red toenails fanning the bed's edge
in preparation for the final stretch.

2

THEIR MEN

Walter

He cut the short grass each week just so the children
could play a game of fair croquet.
The white Chevy he waxed smooth like the silk stockings
worn by young ladies of readiness.
One night, entrenched in a prim society he did not choose,
he drank too much, landing in the city jail.
A secret call made in night's middle to his employer saved
him from experiencing a beating from the lawful, those intent
on making sure the lawless received their just punishment.
Out on bail, he can be seen keeping white folks' yards
polished, his robotic actions a brief respite from the sharp
brutality of jail and the dingy projects.

There's Always Another Train Comin' In

As she watched his penciled form propagate into manhood,
she often imagined his spirit breaking, kaleidoscopic
pieces for the world at large to shake, designing the
course of action he would have to take.
But now she saw tucked underneath the black
overcoat a strength that surpassed their misaligned
assumptions . . . she had loved his blonde curls that
had changed into straight white roads when the Delta
sun refused to blink.

And she loved him now, the conductor's words
"All aboard!" seeming to echo from an array of
faraway places. Since she had always been a
sun-suit in a sandbox to him, she knew he did not
see her reach forward for experiences that could
never be hers. When she scanned the dismembered
magnolia blossoms near the train, she paused, finally
realizing what he had done to her. So when her daddy
voiced, *"There's always another train comin' in,"* she
embraced the kibitzer in spite of herself.

The Doorman

Stately he stood at the hotel arch with an ease
few discover during life, his uniform having
been pressed by his orphaned mother, who
enjoyed tidying up whatever she could, making
the curvaceous creases of his pants line up
faithfully as his tin soldiers used to do.
His silver coat buttons glistened like small
petrified rock pieces, the ones he had observed
in the forest that lay next to his home and a
two-lane highway.
The travelers inside stopped cars were filled
with lusty children, maimed with desires
to grasp what they could and then leave him
agreeably alone, sitting before the creeping kudzu.
So aloneness fit him snugly, those minor
adjustments to the whims of others, gracefully
accepted, so much so that the infrequent
carrying of luggage, or the tipping of his hat
to a stranger were only interludes in a life
content with his exclusiveness, a life that
the persistent Delta sun kept bubbly
warm and far away from a contrived world of
people who execute, brag, and then depart
with an inflated feeling of achievement.

The Ice House

As he sat on the ice house front porch watching everything
but seeing nothing, he shuffled town and went back to the
war days when he felt terrified, yet needed by the government.
His phantom limb ached for adventure, but he could not hatch
from a society that hated black eggs.

When a young girl wearing a cottony Easter bonnet skipped
by him, not daring to stare him in the face, for she had been
taught that his darkness was like a deep-set vicious Delta cloud,
ready to do its dirty work before the cracking sun returned just
so she could dabble near a shade tree with complete trust in
her superiority, he bent his head down instinctively, letting
her pass with illusions intact before continuing to relate the war
stories he repeated to himself to pass the time until his death.

As the child's father opened the ice house door, the black man
did not feel death's cold white fingers strangle him because
he had been a dead man for so long that an encounter with his
physical end could be only a congealed encampment with
death's war correspondent. When he leaned to the side unnoticed,
a black brother in war carried him to the other side.

The Family Reunion

The black elderly people knew why Uncle Frank
came *tilt-a-whirl* drunk to the family reunion
held each year in Aunt Mattie's backyard,
its smooth dirt carved with junk she couldn't let
go because she had never let her husband go
to whom she called the *new* woman in town,
although she had stolen Mattie's husband years ago.

Uncle Frank had let his black skin do him in, because
he was not one to let white folks dictate to him how
to fix bereft cars, for he had lived in junkyards
as a kid, teaching himself the art of car repair.

Today, however, Uncle Frank's jaw seemed to
be so long that his belt could be called a junction.
"Don't the turkey need carving this year?"
he asked unnaturally, his voice quivering unlike
the green Delta leaf that looks so still it becomes
immortal.

When the Boss happened to swirl by in a white
Cadillac, he turned his slim hand over as if it were
the spout of a silver pitcher and waved hearty like,
sticking part of his pin-striped form from the
window to tell everyone Uncle Frank had been
let go. "*Why I got a new little boy that does just
as I say,*" he murmured to the crowd. Uncle
Frank had heard the Boss' exact words before carving
out a canoe in his own body as if he were ridding
the turkey of its dark meat.

At the funeral home, the body designer filled in
the calabash in Uncle Frank's chest with white
cotton bolls from the field, then painted the bolls
a dark brown, a color that bankrupt Uncle Frank's
black body, his bank account having been closed
the day before.

The Covered Bridge

When he courted childhood, the covered bridge
was a fairly hushed collective, a fitting refuge for
one, who when spoken to, lowered his spare visage
pointedly as if he were a broken needle deep-stuck
inside a pincushion.

As a youngster, he thought the covered bridge
green because he misunderstood that there
could be a bottom for an outrageous top.
But the kudzu covered the bridge cinematically,
the leaves continuously rustling, taunting
perfection's home deep within totality.

When he hobbled to the covered bridge for the
last time, an old man with white skin splotches
much larger than when he was a youth, he still ruled
a straightforward cane. He tapped a piece of the
bridge's wood, ants rooting around like piglets in its
crevice; and after the loosened wood slipped to the
ground, so did he.

The Yazoo River

When he sat on a make-believe beach in a stupor,
his red eyes glaring at The Yazoo River, flat and
gray as unkempt aquarium water, the river he split in two
with an imaginary path seemed to mark him as one of its own
permanently, unlike the two sides of an elevator that close
temporarily, carrying its passengers to a planned destination.

If he swam to the other side of the river, he would be in
the same place he left, so why should he even make the effort?
His grandmother, who slipped into black heels with bottoms
shorn to the quick and wore a straw hat on her head out of habit,
even though she had earned the right to stray like a kitten
throughout the well-defined dinginess of her shack, expected
her grandson to stride self-confidently through racist thinking—
gray light bulbs collecting dust within white folks' brains—take
his stand, and be twin-proud for both himself and her.

Why did the dikes have to keep breaking, bending him
to his knees to work through the muck he cared nothing for,
the diabolically tainted water flooding his ambition until it dried
out again, the ambition not pliable within the workings of a
black man's heart intent on plying down the Mississippi River,
the fluid vehicle that could have carried him safely to his dream.

The Tree Stump

The king's green-jeweled crown cropped,
its worried limbs lie across faded red geranium
plants and grass brown-dead from winter's itch.
The tree's concentric circles become a drag
strip for children filled to completion with
simple yard games.
When shadows begin to fleck day into dusk,
the stump seems hidden -
after a gush of darkness rushes toward its
stable shoreline.
Two forms sit, tilted toward each other
for the last time, the lava fires within
their hearts put out by a misunderstanding
that spreads too far.
They depart, the misread collapsing on the
stump like a tired ghost rests on a bed of
black mist.

The Hunch

Each time she saw them they were locked as if they
thrived on being parallel boats in a canal, taking the
ups and downs of life in stride.
Red roses they freely plucked from hidden gardens.
Revealing no creased hint of guilt in their faces, they
boldly crisscrossed their arms, playfully tickling each
other's noses with the fullness of an aroma so many of
the world's attendants dismiss for the realization of
goals not reached, but patched with a continuous
momentum until success is theirs.
She knew the mirage of happiness set before her
would not last, could not last, because the winds
of possessiveness all too soon escalate into powers
naturally uncontrollable, and destructible to one's
sense of self.

She saw the storm coming toward their gelatinous
faces, but she would pick up the pieces and make
him a free man again.

The Drifter

When he swept the town
with a widened vision he
had borrowed from his
grandmother's far-fetched
view of life, he cautiously
watched the townspeople
as they robotic-grooved to
an ancestral beat.

Since he never stayed a
fortnight in a cubbyhole,
he was tempted to leave
immediately, when a baby
girl the color of shallow
night placed a drop cloth
on the palm of his hand.

After she placed a squab
of black tar on the sheet,
he could feel its heat flow
like catsup through his body . . .
he then knew his drifting
days had come to a fitting
close, for he loved the lure
of luster, the challenge of
a blind wizardry.

The Dandelion

When he held the dandelion with his scar-frayed
black hand, he thought about the mussed color of
his childhood: gray innocence. Naivete slipping
from the beginning, spotting, dark destined thoughts
trickling, his rote wishing he could dismiss them . . .
but knowing they held him down like the furry
tarantula, slowly dragging him forward for the
prearranged kill.

Faking nature, he blew the dandelion seeds, who
white-take progress again, leaving him further on
back this time, a catch-up improbable in his lifetime,
but not in his offsprings':
their masterpiece, a coverlet of black made *just so*
for the uproar.

The Conjurer

He's sitting in readiness in a straw chair,
the one he designed with fingers in heat,
magical fingers using a mirror
to traverse the harpies,
the complainers in acute pain
and those bearing life's small annoyances
on their otherwise smooth skin,
those with a team of wart seeds huddled together,
those who want to avoid the physician's long needle.
When his gimmicks work, he's praised,
in company with the gods.
When his efforts fail, he sprawls idle
for a few days on his dirty porch divan.
He's a freak of nature,
resting, waiting,
cuddling a mirror stuffed with magical powers
that steep his system.

The Boarding House

She climbed the wide dark green steps tenuously, for her
left leg hurt from too much competitive running with her
first cousin toward the three-story boarding house.
When she sat down in a tall mahogany chair in front of a
refectory table, she routinely reached for the bowl of
whipped potatoes before the black woman, who practiced
what the girl had been preached, would soon arrive with bowls
of black-eyed peas, carrots, string beans, and skillets of
cornbread.

She hovered over the mashed potatoes like an overly protective
mama since the muddy-eyed, pumpkin-wrinkled men who always
wore overalls would scoop out more than their share if she
didn't see to it that she rescued her proper serving first.
When the banana pudding was brought into the dining room by
the black woman, the rude old men with black dirt caked on
their necks, beckoned the woman to their lower class corner of
the table.

Afraid to disobey anything that resembled stained white, the woman
readily adjusted to their selfish whims, placing massive servings
of banana pudding on their cracked plates.
Although the mollycoddled elementary school child knew she sat
at injustice's terminal, she didn't know that the black woman would
never discover any new connection in a society that's terrain was
under surveillance, the survey sketched in stone.

Peak Teneriffe

It was an early white morning in the Delta, as usual, but no one living
there knew just how white, except the adventurous man clinging to
the wheel of a dark green Nash Rambler on the Peak and his daughter,
her charged personality's motif the potentially dangerous visit to her
daddy's stomping grounds.
The snowflakes, temporary parasites, trembled as they swiftly
covered the revered Indian trail Daddy followed with respect.
Tied behind the car, a red sled bobbled, its bold color capturing
the girl's attention for a spell, just long enough for her to remind
her daddy why they were on the Peak in the first place.
Sensing her impatience, he gradually stopped the car, signaling
her to scan the sled's potential for good or evil.
After she learned the technique of moving like a comfortable
snail, she began to notice her surroundings, the steep dirt
bluffs that hovered over her like ocean cliffs, and the leaves
that ambled across her vision for the purpose of making
her proud that she was secure, well-taken care of by a
society that lived guilt-free, oblivious to anything black,
even the darkened skies that frequently sent benign warnings,
the potential for disaster curling up behind the sun that trimmed
back what nature was trying to teach.

When she first noticed him, his small black body easily filling
the yellow seersucker jumper he wore, she didn't think about
his being in immediate danger, but turned the page in her mind
to a time when she had worn the same jumper as she sat by
the deep purple irises in her back yard while playing with
Beanie Cox, the red plastic doll she had bought at Woolworth's
the day she was permitted by her mother to get a present that
couldn't spoil her birthday or Christmas.
When she looked for the child again, he was standing with
Nurse Rachel, his mother, who ambivalently waved her final
good-bye to a time she had felt secure in her bones, but not in
her heart.

The Broom Pusher

A red wagon rides a broom, the wagon pushed by
witch daddy, a man magically concerned that his
daughter's every whim receive his devoted nod.
They travel down grand avenues, pass Goose Egg
Park, a street canal, and ride over garbage-ridden,
mud-infested roads, where they see roofs dented in
as if nature's Big Dipper decided to scoop out what
topsoil it could, leaving the sordid remains for an
impoverished race of people to sift through.
Father and child experience a quickening, a strong
need to leave the segmented side of small town life,
witch daddy, a fiend for zoning in his daughter's
happiness.

The Message

When I hear the preacher ramble, I know he has to, for
if he hit the mark in my heart, he knows the arrow would
torment the pain that already reigns there, terror's scepter
waving through me to my people, then back again to me.
As the preacher's words dim, I look outside, at the cotton field
that ropes off the horizon, the small white bolls that have felt soft
to my hands for so long, now stinging the sector of my brain that
desires to create. I am the black world's white knight.

I leave the church, high hopes crawling within a distant plan.
As I sit under the oak tree that cranes my house and family, I
see the face in the moon for the first time in my life. The face
is not pasted there, for it could be yanked off like a Halloween
mask. Instead, the face is inset, white within white, inlaid too
far back for a matter-of-fact removal.

The scar tissue so profuse within the face, I fall over,
laughing, glad I'm too weak for the task. Besides,
the boys got plenty of moonshine for me to be
wasting my time solidifying a cause.

Unfortunate Faction

The initial look led to an uncompromising
obsession.
When he wanted out, there was no easy
place for him to root . . .
so he scaled precarious mountain slopes,
swam through a cave's constant night,
burned the desire he had for her in the
desert,
and when he went back to her world,
really, everybody's world, he was not
only free from her but free from any
concept that masked itself just to
seduce him from the plan he had
for himself, a plan that did not have
to fall to the floor like black ink,
seething forward in all directions,
including everyone until the possessive
one used a kerchief to blot out the mass
 . . . thoroughly . . . so that a reflection of
the individual unlike himself would
clearly see what she could become
within the polished wooden floor.

Finding the Key

Inside her heart sits the gray trunk, locked, the
upright purple key, the trunk's mast.
Near the river's bubbles, a steamboat just having passed,
she sinks her small feet into the wet black dirt, moving
her finespun silhouette slightly to leveled ground, the thin
mound of rocks where she sat, too uncomfortable to bear,
the mental pangs coming sharp and steady.

Her daddy had been too good for *him*, riding her on his
slight shoulders when he was too tired from inventory, the
incessant counting of batteries and tires his yearly ritual.

A grove of purple irises lay close by.
She stood up, dusting dry dirt from her white
shorts as she kicked the mud clogs from her feet.
When she reached the irises, it was still broad daylight,
so she had to bend furtively from her knees to sniff
at purple, to everything not upstanding in men.
She'd wear deep purple and white hair inside a cocoon
soon enough.

Soft and light like cabretta, she has infinity at her side
and faith in the appearance of a new specimen.

Ennui

When he scratched his matted
gray hair that looked like the
throw rug on the floor, the only
reminder in his house of his
grandmother, the one who
raised him with the belief
that he was sweet gold, he
cried, not the whimper cry of
a baby, but the hollow cry of
an adult so buried in his pain
that even God would put the last
shovel of dirt on his grave if
He could.

But when he looked out the
dirt-glazed window near the
straw chair where he moaned,
numbed by acts of recognition
that he could have received

if he had been conceived in
a less cautious era, he felt
the heat of the Delta sun's
back on his body, having
been ploughed by misery's
moves, now being embraced
by the sun's warmth as if the
enfant terrible were sending
him anew the final feel of
what he had trod under all
his life.

Cold Colloquy

She knows his heart in the court of law is
passionate as he subjectively collates all
arguments for the win.
She wishes he could be this way with her in
the real world of shadowy feelings felt
next to the hardy oak tree, their childhood friend,
or near the small plants exuding sweat bubbles after
a brief rain, the water beads subservient to the
arrogant heat of summer.
Standing near each other, her mind on him and what
she knows he's thinking, she could be sitting in the
dock as far as he's concerned.
His mind on questions with undefined solutions, her
mind on answers for why their relationship won't work,
won't click like life jacket straps in the open sea,
the sea a welcome escape for his collectible.

Brickyard Hill

Daddy's Nash Rambler, looking like a small loaf of
Colonial bread found in country stores in the fifties,
begins its workout, its shock absorbers doing push-ups,
those pulsating rhythms,
rhythms that abruptly stop, when the summit, a put-on
for a mountain reveals itself.
Rows of shanties, humpbacks on each side of the road,
lend their dusk to the giant yellow sunflowers
crisscrossing dusty yards,
the sunflowers, unapproachable beanstalks for jacks of
no trades.
Black children, like jackstraws, fall in a heap before the
sunflower gods.
One child quietly escapes without disturbing the rest.

3

THEIR CHILDREN

Ruby Red

After china pieces are replaced and scorched sheets,
drapes to diffuse nosy neighbors, are taken inside
to a cool set of chest drawers, the girl, sitting in
front of an oval mirror, begins a Friday night ritual:
caking her thin lips with the darkest color known to the
Maybelline collection at the time, a color she worships
like Mama and apple pie.
Ruby red lipstick, her symbol of girlish freedom, allowed
and encouraged, the world's attempt to keep her innocent of the
purple choker the world wears to appear lovely, but in
a bold actuality is consumed by an untamed hypocrisy.

The Iconoclast

When she was a little girl living in a slightly bent over
shack as if it were on the cutting edge of being
osteoarthritic, she often looked at the cotton fields that
softened the harsh features of her house and wondered
why the fields were called cotton fields instead of sheep fields.
The sheep she had seen were perky white, just like what
she had always known to be cotton.
"Mama, why ain't cotton fields called sheep fields?" she asked
her mother, even though she knew the answer that would
explode from the spiritual baggage her mama toted in her head.
*"Now, Candice Washington, you got to know it's all a part of
Jesus' plan. Everything is only riffraff thinks otherwise."*
Candice would then go touch the cotton bolls, feisty with the
sun's heat, and then mutter to some unknown force that they
felt just like sheep's wool to her.

At school, Candice's quirk-powered questions made her teachers
maliciously confused.
The day Candice questioned a grammar rule located in the tired
and wrinkled language book she studied was the final meddlesome
attack on their jurisprudence. To her English teacher, she was
a conjugation out of control.
*"Candice, you just have to accept that a comma is not used in
short compound sentences because that's the rule. The fact that*

two people have different opinions about what is short or long is irrelevant."

Somehow, the logic of their cases was locked in a small bag with finite dimensions, a bag that couldn't be opened or stretched to accommodate another belonging.

A source of unmitigated dismay for all her teachers, except the young science teacher, Candice retreated to the science lab.

Her science teacher thought her *why* questions genetic mutations in Candice's thinking, part of the evolutionary process, or the leave-taking of childish ways he had heard his own mother say was supposed to happen to all people as revealed in the Scriptures.

The day Mama came to school to see Candice receive a first-place award for her research on the behavior of slime molds in confinement was the happiest day in Mama's life.

Goose Egg Park

Children wag baskets of straw filled with Easter eggs,
the rainbow-colored eggs, informants that the storm
has passed.
Nurses in starched outfits laugh contagiously about
an infectious joke, nurses unable to penetrate another
society's blanched mentality.
The children play innocently, undercover, children making
three-leaf clover necklaces for themselves while one girl
makes a clover ring for her Kewpie doll's wrist.
Children's protected hands push the pulsating waves of
clover to new heights, prompting one of nature's miracles
to surface, the four-leaf clover, a confirmation that faith
does not stay hidden but with its simmering force reigns
supreme.
The park, like a strand, surrounds a penny fountain, the place
where water gushes from a tenacious font, and a penny
tossed means a stratagem comes true.
The children are wont to tire, the caretakers enfold their
trusts, and ready the young for home.

Shadows streak the spot, and a new era emerges.
Clover clods rot; echo peals replace the free-flown laughter.
Waspish hands curtail pennies from the fountain while
water trickles from the spurious fountain spout.
The sporadically thrown disrobed drug needles, a usurer's
dream, storm the water fountain with a contorted necklace.
The fountain's concrete fissures swallow the evil without
a rebuttal.

The Apology

As best friends, we tried on stories for each other.
We let our imaginations take off.
We climbed across truss bridges on the huge sycamore
tree, settling down on one branch to play house.
We didn't see the tuber developing, but its stem
tripped our relationship.
"You can't play with Fran anymore."
The authority figure had neatly tucked in the harsh demand.
"She has tuberculosis and must stay in a sanatorium."
At school, Fran's empty seat, the one in front of me, became
a dust collection.
Doubt balloons were blown and scattered throughout the
community.
"I don't think she will ever return."
The authority figure's words echoed through the vast Tudor
home where all my thoughts with Fran once germinated and
developed.

It was a Delta morning just like the others, hot and thirsty
for activity.
I took my seat at school.
Blonde curls, a small thicket of leftover sawmill swirls, the
ones always tossed to the side, turned toward me.
She was back!

"Let's try on stories for each other," she proffered gently.

She looked cautiously at the face that had become a servant

to cruelty's yoke.

"I can't play with you. You're still sick."

The call to my home still rings, calling my insularity to attention.

"Claire said she couldn't play with Fran anymore. Fran's feelings

are really hurt. Fran's well now."

Her mother's message turned on my mother.

Feeling the verbal onslaught of the savagery that only a parent can

feel, I walked, slowly, fondled by slight dark's oppression, to

Fran's two-story home.

Fran's door knocker squawked at me, a sharp contrast to her mother's

kind voice.

"Won't you come in? It's good to see you again."

Doddering an apology, I tried on my best story for Fran and her parents.

We walked the story line together.

That night Fran and I let our imaginations take off.

In strong dark, we climbed on truss bridges on the huge sycamore

tree, settling down on one branch to play house.

The Adventure

She was one of those oddly constructed children, nervous and active, duly pampered by a host of black nurses her mother had abruptly hired in succession, an act she repeated obsessively because no one liked to be near one of God's mistakes too long: the error might rub off on lives that had already been scrubbed too harshly with a society standing knee-deep in the sandpaper of its fathers.

But Nurse Coreen was as different as late night from early afternoon and didn't care a doodlum squat that the other nurses detested her for being cautiously willing to put up with the 'chil,' as she fondly called her to her confounded face.

Even when the child rubbed rock edges into Coreen's pockmarked skin as a scratch test to see if Coreen could take her crisscrossed antics, Coreen stood tall, fierce with determination that she was going to make something good come out of this obnoxiously skinny child from just another Podunk town. Coreen's brain was a palette knife, always mixing ideas together until one thought emerged with its own special hue.

One late afternoon she swiped the child from devious
concerns, half rolling her up in her large checked apron.
The 'chil' was going on an adventure, but she didn't
know it. When Coreen was a child, she had heard her
grandmother's well stories as they snapped butter beans
in the giant washtubs. Coreen knew the child had never
seen a well, having been served water from silver-tongued
pitchers all her life.

So when Coreen unrolled her starchy apron and propped
the beleaguered child on top of the broken plywood pieces
that smothered the well's potential for evil, the child listened
intently to someone for the first time in her life—to Coreen's
forlorn story about the white masters who had caught what
they thought were black mongrels in white folks' sheets,
throwing the fighting simian forms away into the deep dark
well water.

The Tent Revival

Precisely sitting on staggered, gray concrete blocks inside the tent,
the girls knew they were saved, the recollection of bent knees
touching soft brown church pillows a recent one.
So attending a sawed-off-from-the-norm tent revival was just
another fun thing for them to do, and in this case, like planning
a game of blindman's bluff that would never take place:
What new lesson could they catch from the tent preacher?
When the religious one scuffed through what looked
like sifted sawdust to tell his story, the girls arched their
backs like the proper ladies who were in church at
the other revival, the one being held all week by
a well-known religious leader from the city.

Spun from the preacher's heart, the sermon's
web caught the girls.
Spellbound, they failed to see others jumping
up, one woman fainting on the return, her floral dress
flowers for her grave.
The girls, the last to leave the site, quietly watched
the tent being folded up like a flat wrinkled grocery sack,
the preacher's nose pointed in a new direction,
the Good Book's two sides whipping in the breeze like
a couple of overused black tuxedo flaps.

Spending the Night

I'll swing you near the Redbud tree, where
the children's penny fairy sleeps fitfully,
Mother expectant.
We'll stay up all night, and I'll tell you
stories, not too scary, just goblin-laced.
We'll watch the rabbit crawl down the
hole head first and wonder what kind of
dirt he'll unearth in the magical world
he's entered.
We'll go to The Circle and order fried
chicken with buttered warm biscuits,
walk across Grand Avenue—vagabonds
returning home.
We'll look for four-leaf clovers at Goose
Egg Park but make an out-island border
with a twist of a three-leaf clover necklace.
And your rebuttal?
"I want to go see Mama."

Pilaf

Although she was white as a
Cloroxed dishrag, that old gal
had some meat to her.

When her elderly, yet still
precocious daughter tried to
topple her mama's upper hand,
Mama would step gingerly
toward her makeshift closet,
drag out the red high heels
covered with tiny cobwebs—
you know, the ones that look
like smoke rings stuck on air—
then strut the way she used
to before her daughter had the
verve to vow that depression
had sunk into every sinew of
her mama's frame.

One day when Mama had driven
way past *had it*, she started
scratching her skin, trying to
remove one prominent wart
that had been on her spanking
hand since the conjurer's death.

This action was the partially deaf
Mama's sign to her daughter
to beat it, or she would remove
her from the will and its garden
of codicils.

Old Like Mama

The left hand she touches seems to age with each
movement, but she doesn't protest, for she has
accomplished the goals her mama made it her
business to total up in her child's head, the child's
consent of secondary concern.
A sideways push on her closed hand causes a mountainous
wrinkle to form on one of her knuckles.
But her fingers in forward drive make narrow
rows of cotton fields, just like the ones she
ran up and down to find Mama, who would
shoo her away by saying, *"Why ain't you in
school? You got to get the education I
never got so that you will carry the change,
not make change."*

Lula Mae bowed her head, not wanting to
tell Mama what really happened at school that day.
"Come on child. Let it all out to your mama."
Using the edge of her frayed cotton skirt to

wipe a tear away that was stuck at the side of
her eye like the balloon caught at the edge of the
bedpost at the house, Lula Mae simply stated,
"They moved us to the white school today.
Since there were not enough seats in the classroom,
I was sent away by my new teacher."
Mama knew her brains were half-baked from
too much sun, but she stuck the hoe's handle
deep into the black dirt to practice early on what
pointed comment she would have with her
child's teacher *today* at the new schoolhouse.

Sisters

She sat in a nunnery
just so I could host all blame.
She claimed squatter's rights
when I was up and at 'em.
She wore perfection curls
on the stage while my hair
limped through woods and
streams.
She accidentally stepped on
a spider—then ran to Mama.
I doctored on worms' backs,
straightening out other curvatures
that came my way.
The aging process, a kind mandate
if one is fortunate.
She became a quasar;
I, the salt of the Earth.

Mrs. Stubblefield's Scarecrow

The children gathered around her as she straightened
the crow's blue cap for the final time before she
let the weather's caustic whims determine his destiny.
They watched her as she implanted his body in the
center of the tomato garden, where a flash of dark
brown dirt noticeably existed, untouched by stalks
of tomato vines.
Left defenseless without a care, he thrived, playing
his role to perfection.
After being tossed backwards to the ground by one
of the few winds that dark-roared in the summer,
he began to slip, a true straw man.
When Mrs. Stubblefield went to the field to satisfy the
directive she carried in her brain for the moment,
she quickly bent over, looking intently at the scarecrow,
the special one she had designed to accentuate a child's
features and relieve the tedium from her work-filled days.
Helpless as she was when her first child lay on a thick
white cot so unlike the cotton fields she had known
as a child, the cotton bolls the soft heads of friends she
did not have because she was alone then as now,
she cradled the yellow body in her arms and cried more
than she had before, for not only was her first child dead,
but the scratches from the death of his imitation hurt more.

Miss Delta Doll

Anquilla sat restlessly on the bottom wooden step
of a drove of wooden steps that led to a stooped front
porch.
But she had a growing dream, this black girl from
the Mississippi Delta.
The expected heat of the day had turned into a warm
breeze that kept the heavy black spit curls on her
forehead tepid.

Anquilla had been told by her deep-set relatives that
since she favored Betty Boop, she could be the first
black girl in Calhoun County to win the *Miss Delta Doll*
contest. Anquilla had spied on numerous occasions
a Betty Boop replica on her mother's kitchen counter.
And the unassailable truth of a resemblance between
her and Betty was most apparent to Anquilla also.
Black hair slept snugly on their heads, their torsos were
jealously thin, and Anquilla liked to wear her mother's tall
black heels when they visited her maternal grandmother's
house each Friday night.

The night of the contest, white Barbies lined the stage
like the Hinds Junior College Highsteppers. But those
white girls with the same cotton underwear she had
on were no threat to the bulky dream she had carried
willingly in her head for so long. When she approached
the stage, she could feel what seemed to be cool gasps
of whispers hit her frame before the hot air inside the tent
became reality.

But since Anquilla brought a novel priss and a well-trained
prance to the contest scene, the other girls had to take a
backseat to *Miss Delta Doll.* That night Anquilla slept
comfortably with a non-curtseying smile as the crown lay
primly primped on her bedpost.

Memory

When I looked at my granddaddy's white
clumps of hair on his head, I felt the strong
desire to roam through the cotton fields of my
childhood, where my grandmother hauled
a great big old parachute behind her back—
I guess her way to escape the fields— but I
never did see her escape, except when she
prayerfully sang a sad song—she called it a
dirge—to the spiritual Master, the one who
scanned the fields for black pearls, those
special ones who fell over the line of duty,
but were brought to a feigned life by a
meteor shower of new tasks on the other side.

Handcuffed

As the hot silver circles help sustain the
constraints that have towered over me like
suffocating shadows, I think of Mama's
straw hat, the one she wore in the fields,
yet playfully pulled down over my eyes
so I could not know what lay ahead for
me, a dark cloud in a place that preferred
to live within fluff, a Peter Rabbit world
that turned toward what would reinforce
its throttling thoughts.

The day Mama twirled her tidytiped full
skirt for me to see, I jumped underneath her
protective umbrella, the one that closed
down on me when Mama recalled she had
to be at Miss Floyd's place to cook the
Thanksgiving dinner.

As I rub my fingers together, I think of
cotton days, the times that were soft to
wrestle in with my friends. When death
row beckons its long white arm, I will
trample the cotton field row one final time
to sit in the throne room with God's trinocular
lens focused just on me . . . just on me.

God's Acre

The parched cotton fields purged
the religious thoughts that usually
combed her mind's edges, settling
her down so that her already tough
feet could take it some more.

This time she was rake angry, but
when she pictured her son behind
bars, following the score, her heart
softened, and her vindictive thoughts
turned to mulch, for she had to work to
pay his bail before the night's angers
emerged, taking what respect he
had for himself and stomping it so
far down that he might never have
the energy to retrieve it.

Gentian

Betty Faye's sandbox lay cozily between her
home and her daddy's workshop. There was
both a red roof over her sandbox and a green
door, which opened to the enclosure. One might
say that Betty Faye had a smooth sandbox that
touched all the bases.

The castles she built kept their shapes, even in
old age, for there was no one to intrude upon
her space or change her itinerary.

The day Betty Faye went with her mother to pick
up Nurse Flossie, who had been engaged to do
some ironing and other housework, Betty Faye
glared at Nurse Flossie's child, who was building
castles out of brown sand, or what looked like
sifted dirt. Rubbing her fingers with the flame of
pride, Nurse Flossie's round face studied her child's
productive actions. When the sky delivered a few
tears that later bled gentian, the castles flooded, and
with them the black child's dreams.

Evenness of Tone

When Tameka traced her mother's silky black
skin with a stick of borrowed school chalk, her
mother foot-crushed the chalk into a supple powder
on the dark brown dirt road where they walked.

"I was just trying to make your skin light like mine."
The sun's bright glow seemed to increase in intensity,
shinning gleefully on Tameka's dry beige skin, making
her white like the chalk.

Although the heat was unbearable, Tameka's mother
folded her dove child within bel canto, both mother
and child harmonic, the strands of their ancestry
having already come and gone with the tide.

Digression

She was elderly now, a state of existence she had planned for
others, but not for herself.
When she tugged at the thin, loose strands of white hair that
mocked the thick cotton wig curls she had worn in childhood
plays, she remembered the one time it snowed in the Delta.
As she watched the red plastic cup gradually fill with snow crystals,
she counted each one because she desired to savor the gradual descent
of each unique alignment, newborn snowmen floating parachute free.
Her mother had told her to think of each crystal as a cereal
flake and to stay outside until the inside of the red cup turned white.
When crystals cruised her fingertips, she led them toward the port of call.
The crystals in her cup looked like tiny pieces of a white
mink protea, both fragile as dandelions.
The presence of her mother's dark flesh tones she did not see,
but she could taste the cool white crystals mixed with
french vanilla trickle down her throat, her mother's aphorisms
squirming in her head.
The dizziness subsided before a white calmness obstructed her view.

Danseuse

The ballerina poses within the headstone,
a dull gray outline replacing a past oneness
with pink, both offstage and onstage. The light
flowing dresses she wore as my bambino, she
sacrificed for a consistency of round stiffness,
her leaps and turns demanding this.

Although in a more peaceful place now,
she dances before me here, a piece of
gray gauze seeming to move behind the
cemetery haze that gradually loosens its grip
on the hot, dusky air.

When the dusk dispenses the haze to mystify
another part of the cemetery, her form clarifies
as damsel, truthfulness in the preliminary dark.
I clap for her wild performance until my hands
bruise blue, just as I did many times before for
my damask rose, but I finally accept she's out
of my reach, out of touch with me.

Another Side

He was a leaf that curled up in the night,
unseen, intact, but broken. The places
he did move toward were specks in a
nowhere land. Bottled up like Coke in
its capped glass, he felt the need to
explode, to make a fool of himself in
front of those thin white faces glossed
in stucco, the ones who labored to
forget he existed, fine tuning their
peacock feathers for precise, yet quick
dark blue rebuffs.

The air from their lurid turns choked him,
made him cough up strands of injustice
he left on their cotton field walkways so
that he and the brothers could slither
away into a night of intensity with
words, their map folded, placed into the
lumen where their people had lain for
centuries, suffocating, but forcing them
out on the other side, their throats open
wide, wind gusts no deterrent while
moving toward Jubilee.

One with Shade

When he lies underneath the shade tree of his
youth, the two dark slants meet unceremoniously,
his parade of thoughts having been rained out.

He sees a half-body, most of her lost in the cotton
fields, but he is confident that Mama is trowelling
down her anger, wondering why he is the only fiber
of her flesh who lounges inside the Trojan horse, the
others long gone into worlds they keep up dating.

When Mama looks into one of his eyes, darker than
tree bark, she sees her pupil squandered within
spokes, broken-down treadmills that only he
can rebuild for the chance to be fit.

4

FAITH IN FREEDOM

A Bouquet of Glads

When she moved from Nigeria to the Delta,
the land was so flat that she imagined her
homeland would be seen if she could just
look past the horizon's jealous gaze, its blue
garb no competition for the orange and yellow
wrap she wore.

But what leaned toward her, wrapping her attention,
was a wooden structure part-house, part-hovel,
yet a place she would address home in time.
Kudzu vines had mated on the front porch steps,
their matted irreverence for her need to walk
into her home unencumbered, disregarded.

Yet when she turned her decorative head to the
sound of a gentle rustle, she saw Nigeria in a
black child's squat hands.

When he handed her his bouquet of gladiolus, the
smells of Nigeria slowly crawled back inside her, the
African irises a petite introduction to a culture that would
filter out her similarities to embrace her differences.

Stapelia

Her eyes, blue watercolor dots dropped on a
white saucer, slashing unmercifully through a
person's thoughts, always lit on the aberrant
thought, the one held golden-sacred by the one
who fooled most, but not Louise.

On the side, Louise read palms for pennies to
sustain her meager desires, but she was an
onlooker, not a map-reader by heart.

All adults in her contained community avoided
her, as if her omnipresent eyes were the last
two surviving locusts from a storm that had
devoured their flimsy crops in the past.

When the thunder roared at the townspeople,
Louise added to their horror by intently looking
at each quirk of nature nearest to her as if to
inform them she agreed with the thunder's
message of violent change.

After Louise died, the undertaker brushed
her dried-out strands of black hair away from
her opened eyes, for he knew the ones who
visited closure, twined with Louise . . .
that the softback shells sealing in malformed
thinking were trunks closed permanently until
the new generation would enlighten minds to
switch-on to nature's instructions . . .
and stop pulling up African plants with
putrid-smelling flowers for the weekly bonfire.

The Trip

An archway that refuses to shut. . .
No discrimination here
until Nature erases its view from eyes
still looking for a sign.
Those who pass through its transparent
door will touch a blanched sky, its
blueness stripped of color,
the rainbow, a vibrant diversion
that blinds the senses to an ordinary's
luster.
A quick look backward,
but the colors have vanished.
The dulcet harp still plays with
one's heart,
its quick beat anxiously awaiting the
boomerang's return.

The Kitchen Sink Glass

Delta sun spirals cleanse her glass, the one that
stands unassailable, in its place on the kitchen cabinet
just for her to drink out of and no one else.

She bathed their babies, took the children for
long walks, fed the youngsters applesauce, and
washed the baby boy's blood cuts with their hand
towels.

As she looks at *her* glass for the last time, she
desires to soap it just once, dry it with a jeweler's
cloth, and place it back into the cabinet, where
it's been a cutaway for too long.

Instead she cries, this her last day to be *yeoman*
in the Johnson's home, because she's old
as God, the children are all grown up, and
the rest will be moving to a new one-story flat,
where no maid is needed to scrub the floors,
iron the clothes, or do the dishes—*yet.*

She will hear the yammer in her neck of the
woods, but she won't go back, for the new
place in Xanadu will have the same old glass.

Sittin' Back

She sits in the back of the bus, not cold or hot,
but seething with an injustice the width of
large circular floral designs that have already
taken their seats on her thin print dress just like
the way she's always taken hers, without fuss and
with a stylishly enforced constraint.

She sees the *Walgreen's* sign and recalls
the time she overheard a talcum-powdered
heart pressed into the ways of her society say,
"My daddy uses Blount's dye for his hair,"
to the frayed, brackish skin man with hair
darker than wet licorice—yes, the television
man who gives the same old weather forecast
day after day, for nothing ever changes in the
Delta.

Then the mood hits hard, a punch out, her brain
dead to consequences as her silhouette moves
forward to the empty black seat in the front
of the bus, the one another *Blount's* child has a
fiendish desire for.

The tired look in her eyes will never scar.
She is pushed down the sawed-off escalator
steps all buses have and rides in the backseat
of the police car to jail.

Sinewy

When Sinewy was younger, she was
small and cold as kame and as barren
in her thinking as a karoo.

Yet Mama had bold plans for her
daughter, who was too often
labeled cute, yet unapproachable,
by those in the community that
had surveyed all of its land and
its inhabitants, shaking the jagged
edges from the paper cutouts
thought to be the best of the
community's specimens, these
elaborations intact, yet having
nowhere to grow toward or to
grope for truth, which stayed hidden
in the Delta swamp.

But Sinewy worshiped the swamp,
its cooled-down trees that reached
for forces that only they and Sinewy
could feel, the companion force deep
within her genetic code. It was high
time Sinewy shed timidity, squeezing
the thoughts about freedom from
the genes that had been with her
forever, the ones that had been
shackled until now, her gnome
like nature reaching, swirling,
twisting toward the truths that
the swamp trees, her sisters,
taught her in private.

Presswork

When Mary labored with the iron,
she appeared to be wearing a dark
black glove, for the dark iron and her
brown cashmere skin were one in the
late afternoon dusk on the back porch
of Mother Taylor's home.

We watched her starch-up Paw Paw's
Sunday shirts, and she was a choir
director—yes she was—albeit a stunted
one, for her ironing arm was not as free
to move as high as a choir director's
extensions do, but Mary was free,
wasn't she? She no longer felt prickly
as her forebears had felt in the cotton
fields, so she had to be free.

But we did not see the stings of
past injustices pierce her innermost
thoughts, for we did not know that
Mary had wanted to be a music

director, a bona fide conductor
of a massive orchestra in some big
city up North, but was the one left
behind to sing in her small church's
choir, the one that did not need
a conductor, for the choir voices
sang in harmony and on cue, the
way they had always had to do,
squeaks like the chamois rags
made ignored, just as she had
been forgotten by her family
and given the heave-ho from
society's big old bosom.

Shearing

Although her onion skin revealed
a massive circulatory system in
perfect operation, her sayings
spooked all who rearranged the
few minutes they had to talk
to her.

Even the curtains drooping from
the high ceilings in her home left
nothing to the imagination.

At night when the lamppost
flickered near her living room,
she took joy in traipsing across
the floor in her mint nightgown,
dancing with a past lover some
said.

But the night they saw a cesspool
of shadows streak across her
curtains' rims, they thought she was
dead.

She wasn't though, just sitting on
the back porch fanning the flies
away, smiling profusely, as the
black limbs from the pecan trees
did their dirty work so the
townspeople could call for the
coroner, place her in a casket with
its top open—you know, for every
aristocrat to see the veins protrude
from her forehead and her eyes
roll like two ecumenical pinwheels.

And then they knew the truth: her
tricks were still threshing the chaff
from what was truly golden grain.

The Delta Queen

When she put her dainty, white-gloved hand into her
boyfriend's massive one, she looked directly ahead,
the white object before her, an iceberg on fire.
The drop crystals she wore in her ears looked like
what she imagined The Delta Queen's chandeliers
would in the darkened room where their friends would
be, dancing until the boat's horn took a deep breath
and bellowed out closing time.
She envisioned the black man's saxophone and thought
of pure golden notes threading their way through his
instrument, summoning the boisterous crowd's attention.
The musicians' white tuxedos, fondling the Delta breezes,
would keep things cool, two racial compositions dancing
to the same beats on different spectrums, the spillover
unacceptable tonight, bouffant hairdos falling flat as a flitter
and young ladies' pointed toe shoes staying still, content with
the inevitable change.

But there was no need for the air to be poisoned by sassy
bark tonight: there would be time enough for those ordeals
on the streets and in courts of law.

Nightglow

When the lady had stared too long
at the dark sky and its upstairs sheen,
she covered her eyes with her hands,
for the medley of light sang to her
most wildly conceived desires, a
smorgasbord of what she knew she
would feel, could feel, when she
let herself free-fall into a rosary,
the roses' petals enveloping her with
red, yellow, and purple silks, the
sweet smells combining, producing
the vanilla flavoring she needed to
sweeten the prejudiced ones, the ones
who never look up to see how much
light the dark wears, its closely knit
jeweled necklace, a glint spark of
its genuine worth.

Cream of the Crop

Since Camphor repeatedly tripped over her mother's long
brown sack dress out in the cotton fields, everyone
guessed she had a limp, a deformity she would not
outgrow, being punched with the Delta sun's
tortuous ropes that had already wrung out the
most seasoned workers on the black dirt roads
next to the cotton fields.

When she analyzed the cotton bolls she would
lay down in neatly partitioned rows, she thought
of her grandfather and his friends, the weary ones
who mimicked really old people like weepy Aunt
Ruby, whose hair was so dry and distraught that
her daughters could never get it balled up in one
piece, one gray strand always sticking its tongue
out at them.

One day Camphor began to follow the cuffed edge
of a desire she had pressed down so long that it
shined before her eyes.

Stepping out of her dress like a well-proportioned
sack of flour, she painted her toenails red, combed
her black hair dead flat, and wore her sister's
new town dress to the red brick Annie Ellis
Elementary School where the white children
went, taking a front row seat next to the boy
who had measles perennially.

Camphor's mother was at the police station by
the length of the sawmill whistle to release
the *cream of the crop*, her one and only who
had the audacity to begin a taffy pull that
would go from sea to shining sea.

Poppycock

When Mama heard me talk crazy like,
she removed her straw hat from her
head, the hat that had artificial flowers
on it that matched every step in the rainbow,
and told me to quit talking malarkey—
for she said that the silly halftime words
would get me nowhere, just bring me down
to the level of the other black folks who
talked trash 'cause they had nothing better to
do than beat their gums down so far that
their wide-opened mouths looked as empty
as a cleaned-out sewage tank.

So when I wanted to trash-talk, I snuck
into the deepest recesses of the woods,
the place no intelligent person would be
seen because the mud-roots there could roll
your feet up into their quicksand and not
let go.

It would be soon enough to let the
poppycock die, once and for all,
from my breath that seemed to get
right strong from holding up those
big words Mama said I would know
one day.

Magnolia Girl

You are like the magnolia bloom, soft, pure,
stilled within hunter green.
You are most happy facing the sun,
embracing her light, but unsuccessful in using
her gift to thaw frozen tensions.

In middle age when blossoms curl, you begin
a descent toward cupped hands of the
downtrodden, blending dainty blood with
rich blood, a decisive color not found
where lie the pallid:
in shrunken forts near gray marble.

Laurels

In the small town, where everyone sat in a circle not welcoming
outsiders, she was the preeminent one, habitually used to receiving
the accolades the townspeople thought worthy for their narrow attention.
Some maliciously thought she garnered the awards because her daddy
had died when she was not far removed from the nascent stage.
So when she began to wear dresses with necklines too low for the
town's mores, biting words flowed with ease, for wasn't it the
appropriate action to take for one who wouldn't readily conform to
the town's whimless standards?
Since Jesus had died on the cross, the town's residents thought she
should be grouted, not literally, of course, but required to suffer in
ways their pinpointed minds could devise.
They knew that mental sufferings traveled longer distances
than physical ones, *and so did she.*
Feeling the ripple of injustice begin to
surface in her senses, she narrowly escaped
their namby-pamby retributions by sitting
on the courthouse square bench revered by
the town's dwarf elders and wearing Puritan
attire on the most lawless day of the year,
the day when the townspeople misplaced
their heirloom ways and went to the county fair.

In Reverse

She bumps into a prior time,
the present too much of an orthodox
hassle for humanity.
The sudden stop causes leafy
green tree sprouts to quiver with
an anticipation that highly correlates
with hers.
What she did as a child she
miraculously repeats.
Sprawled out in a field of clover that's
sticky wet with the flowing newness
of dawn, she feels her rough, tanned skin
tickled brazenly, her skin having been
tarnished by a barren, unstable world that
turns its attention to city life, where the
misguided share too freely a wealth
of misinformation.

She's a baroness of pleasurable thoughts,
the newness of the old peeling off
layers her physical presence had
accumulated over time
from a world bent on a
repetitious covering
of stale hypocrisies
on *both* the audacious and the reticent.
When she leaves, she stays.

Incognito

A tree in spring, changing from buds to leaves,
finds its identity in winter.
On Halloween night innocence travels inside black
capes and white slippers.
Passionate love beats underneath a Santa Claus suit.
Pillow feather feelings capture heart space in the
most obdurate person.
A woman, her purple cotton dress sticky wet, sits
inside a country church, hum-suffering and waving a
Jesus fan,
her faith, a mystery in a world that while spinning,
twists hate plaits on the loom.

Ignescent

She cashed her usual bumpy walk to sizzle with the roses
on fire.
She had always thought the red roses so like her, their
wet petals in heat.
What use to qualm through life's perplexities without
bold intensity, red's symbol?
She had an infectious knack for traveling straight to
the verve of flawed dictators,
burning their stagnant hands with word slights
just so they'd get the hint,
untangle their jeopardizes,
and live concomitantly
on the sultry plane with the heretical.

In Dutch

She cries uncontrollably underneath the
newly formed leaves,
light green leaves, which if thumb-stroked
would wet-fold,
closing abruptly, with no open ends
like a slim tube one might find in a lab.
Immobile within a constraint
that quickly and defiantly
makes itself perpetually
felt, the young woman in pain pushes hard
to forget her past.
Claws digging in, she
has her way, quietly leaving
a deep concern that fades into her past.
She stands with freedom at her side,
rush groping as many newly formed leaves
as she can, in the allotted time,
tossing them upward, but patiently waiting
for their return to her,
someone who needs a soft touch
to offset the austere, chilled cuffs
that will be placed on her rough hands
by the brawny woman who strides confidently
toward her.

Fine White Gloves

Cradled fetus like, a dolt in her mother's eyes,
she dreamed her dark black hands melted inside
the fine white gloves the fine white women
of the town wore.

Her hands, softer than the cotton bolls she picked
each day from green shells, was a restful feel,
one she knew nothing of in flesh-life because
she looked like coal from the despised northern
factories, so dense-dark that the comstock of the town
dismissed the possibility that she and her mama were
attired in black, but glowing red inside.

When she awakened, she was born the second time,
for when she stretched out her tiny terrestrial hand
against her mother's more massive fingers, she cast
a baronial promise to the world that as she grew, she
would travel in directions her mother had beheaded
in her dreams long ago.

Down the Dirt Road

This time she spread her time walking down the
dirt road, full palming the yellow wildflowers
gently, as naturally as she always combed her already
smooth blonde hair, each strand a replica of the
long dirt road.

When she saw nestled in connected thick grass patches
scrambled boards that used to be her house in that
faraway land some call childhood, she knew she
was home, the place she could scratch the meaning
of life from, and take the fire back to her other
home in the city, a place tossed like salad greens.
When she decided to return to a simpler time, she went
near the place where her mother had kept extra Christmas
gifts on a shaky cardboard table in the back bedroom,
just so a child at the back door with a gift for her

daughter would not go home empty-handed.
Even the cards were signed by Mother, who pretended
to have a child's hillside signature, while the innocent ones
spied honesty in each other's faces, the back screen door
hiding evil on the hinges.

Although the smoldering ashes in her heart had been
emerald green for too long, she felt the giant rush of emotion
that would foreclose on oblivion and thrust her toward the
image of a new kind of life she would be a beggar for.

Chemise

Although the lady's form was as long
as the Mississippi River without its
curves, this knowledge did not burst
the well-contrived bubbles that filled
her head, each bubble restraining its
own stereotype from taking on any
novel views about the world.

The lady reinforced her straight-laced
thinking each day by wearing chemise
dresses, black on Sundays, for there was
usually a funeral to attend, and white on
Mondays, for she had never heard of
a wedding occurring on Monday—
and God forbid, she ever marry.

The day she saw a black man hunched
over dead like a stained cotton boll,
she went to stand over him like a
tall sycamore tree, so that at least
in death he could have some shade,
some relief from the Delta's heat.

When the undertaker arrived, scooping
him up with a brown shovel the way
she remembered her own mama
scooping brown sugar from a bin, all of
the bubbles in her head began to leak,
the stereotypes she had protected for
ages running rampant like scalded dogs,
dogs her grandmother used to tell her
stories about with the ghosts she freed
each time she peeked underneath one
of her doilies on end tables, each doily
a home for one of Grandmother's flaccid
ghosts, the ones that elongated each
time Grandmother stretched out a tale.

A Readiness for Life

Not alone in a deep spring sleep,
a distant light becomes my girth.
The white glare of a porcelain bathroom
heater heats my senses, my father's head
propped against the impending white wake.
My mother's trembling fingers reach for the
phone, a rhetorical shroud.
I reach for a bath cloth, cooled by water, my
mind cut into petit fours by the doctor's instructions.
I touch the gradually receding form with the cool cloth,
or should it have been a warm cloth?
A twitch, a response, shuffles my emotions.
I pull the card of life and leave the bathroom.
I go to my daddy's bed, his pillow's hollow place
reminding me of an overturned sombrero.
I lie next to his pillow before the doctor arrives.
He feels a wrist but no pulse.
"Gwen, Brownie is dead."

The words initiate in me unexpected reflexes.
To stop the choking sensations, I pull the image of
an oxygen tent up over my body, the cover I had
seen in the hospital room every afternoon after school.
I push my head into the pillow next to his and cry enough
to buoy a daughtership of pain.
I turn to look at the incessant smile on my Kewpie doll's face,
a premonition of things to come.

Basilica

Basilica walked through fall leaves
of historical significance because
the massive piles of yellows, reds,
and browns had been in this neck of
the woods for a century, since she had
heard her great-grandmother refer
to them while she hand-raked the silver
strands of hair that had fallen on her
face backwards, then clipped the
unruly strands with a clothespin.

Since Basilica was taller than the
other women her age, it was not that
hard for her to envision a vast change
that would have to be swashed through
the society she knew, the one that let
justice wince at freedom extorted.

As Basilica continued to step on
the wood's thick flooring, she
paused, then stepped onto a tree
stump to tell the butterflies, dry
leaves hovering, that the victory
was way out there, bubbling within
minds scot-free.

About the Author

CLAIRE T. FEILD was born and grew up in Yazoo City, Mississippi, the town where the hills meet the Mississippi Delta. She has been a children's librarian, a high school English teacher, a newspaper feature writer, an editor and publisher for a national literary journal *Beyond Doggerel,* a writer for professional education journals, and a lecturer in English at Tuskegee University. She is currently an English instructor at Southern Union Community College in Opelika, Alabama. Nominated for a Pushcart Prize by *Krater Quarterly* in 2001, she continues to publish poetry extensively in literary journals and anthologies such as, *Apostrophe: USCB Journal of the Arts; Folio: A Literary Journal of the American University; The Mochila Review; Smartish Pace; Neovictorian/Cochlea; Sophie's Wind; Knowing Stones: Poems of Exotic Places; Noccalula; Mediphors; The Eclectic Woman; Indigenous Fiction; Bloodstone Stanislaus Poetry Anthology; Potpourri: A Quarterly International Magazine; Big Muddy: A Journal of the Mississippi River Valley; Aura; Carriage House Review;* and *Buffalo Woman's Vision.*

Mississippi Delta Women in Prism is her first book.